PREFACE

Preface:

Welcome to "Secure Transactions: The Fundamentals of PCI DSS." In this book, we embark on a journey into the complex yet vital world of payment card security and the Payment Card Industry Data Security Standard (PCI DSS). As the digital landscape evolves and electronic payments become the norm, the need for robust security measures has never been more crucial. The protection of sensitive cardholder data and the establishment of a secure transaction environment are paramount for businesses of all sizes.

At its core, this book aims to demystify the intricacies of PCI DSS and provide a comprehensive understanding of its fundamental principles. We believe that knowledge is power, and by equipping businesses, professionals, and security enthusiasts with a solid understanding of PCI DSS, we empower them to make informed decisions and implement effective security measures.

The journey begins with an exploration of the evolution of electronic payments and the rapid growth of digital transactions. We examine the risks associated with these transactions and the need for a standardized framework that ensures security, integrity, and confidentiality. From there, we dive into the heart of PCI DSS, meticulously dissecting each of its twelve requirements, unraveling their significance, and providing clear explanations supported by real-world examples.

However, this book is not solely about deciphering technical requirements. It is about fostering a holistic security mindset that permeates every aspect of your organization. We delve into risk management strategies, incident response planning, and the creation of a culture of security that extends beyond compliance. Our aim is to inspire you to view security as an ongoing commitment and a shared responsibility across your entire organization.

Throughout this book, we emphasize the practical aspects of implementing PCI DSS compliance. We provide actionable guidance, highlighting best practices, and sharing tips to help you navigate the challenges that may arise. By demystifying the compliance validation process and offering insights into common pitfalls, we strive to equip you with the tools necessary to achieve and maintain compliance.

We must acknowledge that achieving PCI DSS compliance is not a one-time task but an ongoing journey. Technology evolves, threats emerge, and standards adapt. Therefore, it is vital to stay informed, remain vigilant, and continuously reassess and enhance your security measures.

Whether you are a business owner, an IT professional, a compliance officer, or someone passionate about the security of payment transactions, this book serves as your trusted companion. We encourage you to embrace this knowledge, implement the best practices shared within these pages, and make a tangible difference in safeguarding sensitive cardholder data.

We hope that "Secure Transactions: The Fundamentals of PCI DSS" provides you with the insights, guidance, and inspiration you need to protect your customers, enhance your security posture, and foster a culture of trust in today's digital economy.

Let's embark on this journey together.

Sincerely,

Ethan Damitier

CHAPTER 1

The History of PCI DSS

The payment card industry has been around for decades, but it has evolved significantly over the years. What began as a simple way to facilitate purchases with credit or debit cards has become a highly regulated and multifaceted industry. In the 1950s, the first payment cards were introduced as charge cards by BankAmericard, now known as Visa, and American Express. These cards allowed customers to pay for goods and services without having to use cash. This was a revolutionary concept at the time, as it allowed consumers to avoid having to carry a large amount of cash. In the 1970s, the concept of credit cards was introduced.

These cards allowed consumers to borrow money to make purchases, with the expectation that they would pay it back over time, typically with interest. This was a major advancement and made credit cards popular among consumers. In the 1980s, debit cards were introduced. These cards allowed customers to access their own money from their bank accounts, but without having to carry around a large amount of cash. This was an even more convenient way for consumers to make purchases, as they no longer had to worry about carrying large sums of money. In the 1990s, the payment card industry began to shift towards electronic payments. This included the introduction of automated teller machines (ATMs), which allowed customers to access their bank accounts without having to go to a bank. It also included the introduction of online payments, which allowed customers to make purchases with their credit or debit cards without having to physically present the card.

Today, the payment card industry is highly regulated and continues to evolve. Many payment cards now offer additional features such as rewards programs, loyalty programs, and security features. This has allowed customers to use their cards in a more secure and convenient manner. In addition, the industry has seen the emergence of virtual cards, mobile wallets, and cryptocurrency, which are all changing the way we make payments. The Payment Card Industry (PCI) Data Security Standard (DSS) was created to ensure that organizations that process, store, and transmit payment card data protect their customers' data from unauthorized access. As the use of payment cards and the number of transactions that involve them have grown over the years, so has the need to protect the data associated with these cards. The PCI DSS was developed by the Payment Card Industry Security Standards Council, which is comprised of the five major payment card brands: American Express, Discover, JCB, MasterCard, and Visa. The PCI DSS was created to ensure that organizations that process card payments utilize strong data security measures to protect the customer's data. These measures include encrypting cardholder data, restricting access to cardholder data, developing secure applications, implementing strong access control measures, and regularly monitoring and testing their security systems.

The PCI DSS requires organizations to report any security breaches, and to comply with the standard, they must regularly assess their compliance with the requirements and submit the results to a Qualified Security Assessor (QSA). The QSA is responsible for verifying that the organization is in compliance with the standard and will issue a report that outlines any areas where the organization is not in compliance. Organizations are also required to undergo regular security scans to identify any vulnerabilities in their systems. These scans are performed by an Approved Scanning Vendor (ASV) and are designed to detect any weaknesses in the organization's security systems. The PCI DSS is designed to protect cardholder data and ensure that organizations are adhering to best practices when it comes to data security. By complying with the standard, organizations can protect their customers' data and help to ensure that their data is secure and not at risk of being compromised.

The Payment Card Industry Data Security Standard (PCI DSS) is a set of security standards that are designed to ensure the security of credit card and debit card information. It was created by the major credit card companies, including Visa, Mastercard, American Express, Discover, and JCB, in order to protect cardholders and merchants from data breaches and other cyber threats. The PCI DSS is a comprehensive set of requirements that covers all aspects of cardholder data security, from storage and transmission to access control and network security. The PCI DSS was first released in 2004 and has been updated several times since then, most recently in 2018. The standard is designed to be flexible enough to be implemented by organizations of all sizes, from large enterprises to smaller businesses. The standard applies to any organization that processes, stores, or transmits cardholder data, including merchants, service providers, payment processors, and data centers.

The PCI DSS is organized into six main areas of focus, each with its own set of requirements. These include:

1. *Network Security*: This includes requirements for firewalls, data encryption, and other measures to protect cardholder data as it is transmitted over the network.

2. *Access Control*: This includes requirements for access control measures, such as user authentication, authorization, and logging.

3. *Data Integrity*: This includes requirements for ensuring the accuracy and completeness of cardholder data.

4. *System Maintenance*: This includes requirements for ensuring the availability and integrity of systems and cardholder data.

5. *Monitoring and Testing*: This includes requirements for regular monitoring and testing of systems and cardholder data.

6. *Physical Security*: This includes requirements for protecting cardholder data in physical locations.

The PCI DSS also includes requirements for other related security measures, such as security policies, vendor management, and incident response. Organizations must comply with the PCI DSS in order to accept payments from major credit cards. Non-compliance can result in large fines and other penalties. The PCI DSS is a comprehensive set of requirements that cover the entire lifecycle of payment card data, from the time it is collected to the time it is destroyed. It requires organizations to have processes and procedures in place to protect cardholder data and ensure its security. This includes encryption, authentication, and access control measures. Additionally, organizations must regularly monitor and test their networks to ensure they are compliant with the PCI DSS. Organizations that process, store, transmit, or accept payment card information must comply with the PCI DSS in order to remain compliant with the major credit card companies. Failure to comply with the PCI DSS can result in fines and other penalties.The PCI DSS is organized into six main areas of focus, each with its own set of requirements. Compliance with the PCI DSS is essential for any organization that processes cardholder data.

Overall, the payment card industry has come a long way since its inception in the 1950s. As technology continues to advance, the industry is likely to evolve even further in the future. In summary, the Payment Card Industry Data Security Standard is a comprehensive set of security requirements designed to protect cardholder data and reduce the risk of data breaches. The standard applies to any organization that processes, stores, or transmits cardholder data, and organizations must comply with the standard in order to accept payments from major credit cards.

CHAPTER 2

Introduction

Overview of the 12 Requirements of the PCI DSS

The Payment Card Industry Data Security Standard (PCI DSS) is a set of security requirements designed to protect cardholder data and ensure its security. It is a global standard that applies to any organization that processes, stores, transmits, or accepts payment card information. It was developed by the Payment Card Industry Security Standards Council (PCI SSC) and is a requirement of the major credit card companies such as Visa, MasterCard, Discover, and American Express. The PCI DSS is intended to protect organizations from potential data breaches and provides a framework for organizations to build secure systems and processes.

The PCI DSS is composed of twelve requirements, divided into six categories:

- Build and Maintain a Secure Network
- Protect Cardholder Data
- Maintain a Vulnerability Management Program
- Implement Strong Access Control Measures
- Regularly Monitor and Test Networks
- Maintain an Information Security Policy

These requirements are designed to ensure organizations have the necessary measures in place to protect cardholder data and to prevent data breaches.The Payment Card Industry Data Security Standard (PCI DSS) is a set of security requirements developed to protect cardholder data and to ensure the secure handling of credit and debit card transactions. It is applicable to any organization, regardless of size, that processes, stores, or transmits cardholder data.

CHAPTER 3

The 12 Requirements of the PCI DSS

1. Maintain a secure network: This requirement includes the installation and maintenance of firewalls and other security measures to protect cardholder data. This includes regularly testing the security systems and processes, and implementing access control measures.

Explanation:

The Payment Card Industry Data Security Standard (PCI DSS) is a set of industry-wide security standards designed to ensure that all organizations that process, store, or transmit cardholder data maintain a secure environment. The PCI DSS sets out twelve requirements for organizations to comply with in order to protect cardholder data and ensure the security of transactions.

Requirement 1 of the PCI DSS is "Install and maintain a firewall configuration to protect cardholder data." This requirement is designed to ensure that organizations protect their cardholder data by implementing appropriate technical controls. Firewalls are a key tool for protecting cardholder data as they provide a barrier between the organization's internal network and any external networks, such as the internet. Firewalls are configured to allow only the types of traffic that are necessary for the organization's operations, while blocking any other traffic. This ensures that only authorized users are able to access the organization's cardholder data. Organizations must implement and maintain a firewall configuration that includes the following elements:

- Network segmentation: This means that the organization's internal network is segmented into different zones, each of which is assigned different levels of access. This allows the organization to protect sensitive areas of their network, such as cardholder data, from unauthorized access.

- Network traffic monitoring: Organizations must monitor incoming and outgoing network traffic to ensure that only authorized traffic is allowed.

- Access control: Access control measures must be in place to ensure that only authorized users are able to access the organization's cardholder data.

- Encryption: All sensitive data must be encrypted to ensure that it is secure and cannot be accessed by unauthorized users.

Organizations must also regularly review their firewall configuration to ensure that it is still effective and up to date. Any changes to the configuration must be documented and approved by the appropriate personnel. By implementing and maintaining a firewall configuration to protect cardholder data, organizations will be able to ensure the security of their transactions and comply with the PCI DSS.

2. *Requirement 2 of the PCI DSS* is "Protect cardholder data": Organizations must protect cardholder data both in transit and at rest. This includes encrypting data and using strong access

control measures to limit access to cardholder data.

Explanation:

The Payment Card Industry Data Security Standard (PCI DSS) is a set of security standards established by the Payment Card Industry Security Standards Council (PCI SSC) to help protect customer data when processing, storing, or transmitting payment card information. Requirement 2 of the PCI DSS focuses on the protection of cardholder data. This requirement mandates that organizations take steps to protect cardholder data stored electronically, transmitted electronically, or printed on paper. To comply with this requirement, organizations must implement the following measures:

1. Use appropriate encryption technologies like TLS and SSL to protect cardholder data when it is being transmitted over public networks, including the Internet, or in wireless environments.

2. Use firewalls to restrict access to cardholder data within the organization's systems.

3. Restrict access to cardholder data by only giving access to those individuals who have a legitimate business need to know.

4. Monitor and control access to cardholder data by implementing measures such as user authentication, training, and secure access terminals.

5. Implement physical security measures, such as video surveillance, locks, and restricted access to data processing areas.

6. Perform regular penetration tests and vulnerability scans to

identify and address any potential vulnerabilities.

7. Implement a secure configuration policy for all systems, applications, and networks.

8. Establish and maintain an information security policy to ensure that all employees are aware of their responsibilities regarding the security of cardholder data.

By implementing these measures, organizations can ensure that cardholder data is adequately protected from unauthorized access. These measures are essential for organizations to comply with the Payment Card Industry Data Security Standard and to protect the security of their customers' data.

CHAPTER 4

Maintain a vulnerability management program: Organizations must have a program in place to identify and address vulnerabilities in their system. This includes regularly running vulnerability scans and patching any identified vulnerabilities.

Explanation:

The Payment Card Industry Data Security Standard (PCI DSS) is a set of security requirements designed to ensure that all companies that accept, process, store, or transmit credit card information maintain a secure environment. The PCI DSS was developed by the Payment Card Industry Security Standards Council, a body of security experts from the major credit card companies. Requirement 3 of the PCI DSS focuses on the protection of cardholder data.

Requirement 3 of the PCI DSS requires that companies protect cardholder data by implementing strong access control measures. This includes limiting access to cardholder data both physically and logically. To limit physical access to cardholder data, companies must use appropriate facility entry controls to restrict access to authorized personnel. These controls may include the use of locks, alarm systems, video surveillance, and other physical security measures. Additionally, companies must securely dispose of media containing cardholder data when it is no longer needed for business purposes. To limit logical access to cardholder data, companies must implement strong access control measures. This includes assigning a unique ID to each person with access to cardholder data, restricting access to cardholder data to only those individuals who need it to perform their job duties, and monitoring access to cardholder data. Companies must also ensure that all passwords are kept secure and are changed at least every 90 days.

To protect against unauthorized access to cardholder data, companies must also implement strong user authentication measures. This includes using multi-factor authentication for remote access to cardholder data and implementing additional security measures, such as token authentication, to protect against unauthorized access to cardholder data. Finally, companies must also implement strong network security measures. This includes regularly testing and monitoring networks for vulnerabilities, using firewalls and intrusion detection systems to protect against unauthorized access to cardholder data, and implementing appropriate encryption technologies to protect cardholder data.

In summary, Requirement 3 of the PCI DSS requires companies to implement strong access control measures to protect against unauthorized access to cardholder data. This includes limiting physical access to cardholder data, limiting logical access to cardholder data, implementing strong user authentication measures, and implementing strong network security measures.

4. *Requirement 4 of the PCI DSS* is implement strong access control measures: Organizations must implement strong access control measures to limit access to cardholder data. This includes implementing unique user IDs and passwords, and the use of multi-factor authentication.

Explanation:

The Payment Card Industry Data Security Standard (PCI DSS) is a set of security requirements designed to ensure that all organizations that accept, process, store, or transmit credit card information maintain a secure environment. Requirement 4 of the PCI DSS focuses on the secure management of sensitive cardholder data. The objective of Requirement 4 is to ensure that organizations securely manage cardholder data, including the creation, storage, transmission, and disposal of the data. This requirement outlines a number of controls and processes that must be implemented in order to ensure the secure management of cardholder data. Organizations must first identify the types of cardholder data they collect and store. This includes anything that can be used to identify a cardholder, such as cardholder name, account number, expiration date, and security code. Organizations must also establish and maintain secure access control measures for all systems that store, process, or transmit cardholder data. This includes the implementation of access control measures such as user authentication and authorization, and the use of cryptographic techniques to protect cardholder data.

Organizations must also establish a secure data encryption policy for the transmission of cardholder data across public networks. This includes the use of secure protocols such as Transport Layer Security (TLS) or Secure Socket Layer (SSL). Organizations must also implement secure data storage measures, such as the use of firewalls to protect cardholder data from unauthorized access. Organizations must also ensure that cardholder data is securely disposed of when no longer needed. This includes the use of secure deletion techniques such as overwriting or degaussing. Organizations must also develop and maintain a secure information disposal policy and ensure that employees are properly trained on the policy.

Finally, organizations must monitor and test their security systems and processes to ensure that cardholder data is securely managed. This includes the use of vulnerability scans, penetration tests, and other security tests to ensure that all security measures are functioning properly.These are the basic requirements of Requirement 4 of the PCI DSS. Organizations must ensure that they are compliant with this requirement in order to maintain a secure environment for the processing and storage of cardholder data. Failure to comply with this requirement can result in significant fines and penalties.

5. *Requirement 5 of the PCI DSS* is regularly monitor and test networks: Organizations must regularly monitor and test their networks to ensure the security of cardholder data. This includes running regular scans and tests, and implementing corrective measures to address any identified issues.

Explanation:

The Payment Card Industry Data Security Standard (PCI DSS) is a set of security standards designed to protect organizations that process, store, or transmit cardholder data. Requirements 5 of the PCI DSS focuses on access control measures. This requirement ensures that organizations have logical and physical access control measures in place in order to protect cardholder data from unauthorized access. Organizations must implement access control measures that are specifically designed to restrict access to cardholder data based on the individual's role in the organization. This means that cardholder data must be accessible only to individuals who need it to perform their job duties. Organizations must also document and implement policies and procedures for granting and revoking access to cardholder data. Organizations must also have a system in place to monitor access to cardholder data. This includes logging access attempts, both successful and unsuccessful, to cardholder data. Organizations must also have a process in place to regularly review logs for any suspicious activity.

Organizations must also implement processes to protect authentication credentials, such as user IDs and passwords, that are used to access cardholder data. This includes implementing a policy for changing passwords after a certain period of time, as well as prohibiting the sharing of credentials. Organizations must also implement physical access control measures to protect cardholder data. This includes restricting physical access to cardholder data by implementing access control systems, such as locks, gates, ID cards, and video surveillance. Organizations must also ensure that physical access is only granted to individuals who have a legitimate need for access. Lastly, organizations must implement processes for securely disposing of cardholder data. This includes securely deleting or destroying cardholder data when it is no longer needed. Organizations must also have a process in place to ensure that cardholder data is securely disposed of when it is no longer needed.

In summary, Requirement 5 of the PCI DSS focuses on access control measures. Organizations must implement access control measures that are specifically designed to restrict access to cardholder data based on the individual's role in the organization. Organizations must also have a system in place to monitor access to cardholder data, protect authentication credentials, implement physical access control measures, and securely dispose of cardholder data.

CHAPTER 5

6. *Requirement 6 of the PCI DSS is* Maintain an information security policy: Organizations must have an information security policy in place that outlines the security measures and processes that must be implemented in order to protect cardholder data.

Explanation:

The Payment Card Industry Data Security Standard (PCI DSS) is a set of security requirements designed to protect cardholder data and ensure the secure handling of credit and debit card transactions. Requirement 6 of the PCI DSS focuses on the secure development of applications. It states that all applications must be securely developed in accordance with industry standards and best practices. Secure application development is an important part of any security strategy and is required for any organization that uses, stores, processes, or transmits cardholder data. Requirement 6 of the PCI DSS provides specific guidance on how to meet this requirement. It includes requirements for developing and maintaining secure applications, including:

1. Establish secure coding guidelines and ensure that all applications developed for use in the environment meet those guidelines.

2. Perform regular security code reviews to identify any potential security vulnerabilities.

3. Ensure all code changes are tested and approved before deployment.

4. Ensure that all applications are subject to vulnerability scans and security testing prior to deployment.

5. Ensure all code changes are tracked and recorded.

6. Ensure that all applications are regularly monitored for security vulnerabilities and any issues are addressed promptly.

7. Ensure that all applications are subject to penetration testing prior to deployment.

8. Ensure that all applications are subject to regular security reviews to assess the impact of any potential changes or vulnerabilities.

The purpose of Requirement 6 is to ensure that all applications developed for use in the environment are secure and adequately protected from malicious attackers. By following these requirements, organizations can ensure that their applications remain secure and compliant with the PCI DSS.

7. Restrict access to cardholder data: Organizations must have controls in place to restrict access to cardholder data. This includes implementing access control measures and regularly monitoring access to cardholder data.

Explanation:

The Payment Card Industry Data Security Standard (PCI DSS) is a set of data security regulations that all companies that store, process, or transmit cardholder data must adhere to. Requirement 7 of the PCI DSS is focused on ensuring secure systems and applications are used. This requirement is intended to protect cardholder data from attack by malicious software, such as viruses, worms, and Trojans.

Requirement 7 mandates that organizations must maintain systems and applications that are secure and up to date. Specifically, organizations must:

1. Develop and maintain secure systems and applications.

This includes an ongoing process of identifying and mitigating vulnerabilities in systems, applications, and processes. Organizations should regularly review their systems and applications for potential weaknesses and vulnerabilities, and take steps to remediate any issues that are identified.

2. Ensure that all system components and software are protected from known vulnerabilities by installing applicable security patches.

Organizations should have a process in place to ensure that all systems and applications are regularly updated with the latest security patches. Systems and applications should be tested to ensure that the patches are properly applied and functioning as intended.

3. Implement a process for secure development and testing of all in-house developed or acquired applications.

Organizations should have a process in place to ensure that any applications developed in-house or acquired from third-party vendors are secure. This process should include reviews and tests to check for potential vulnerabilities.

4. Maintain a secure network architecture.

Organizations should have a secure network architecture in place to protect cardholder data. This includes implementing firewalls to protect against unauthorized access, authentication and access controls, and logging and monitoring systems.

5. Implement an antivirus solution.

Organizations should have an antivirus solution in place to protect against malicious software. This includes regularly updating virus definitions and scanning systems and applications for viruses and malware.

By adhering to Requirement 7 of the PCI DSS, organizations can ensure that their systems and applications are secure and up to date. This can help protect cardholder data from attack by malicious software, and help organizations maintain compliance with the PCI DSS.

8. *Requirement 8 of the PCI DSS* Regularly monitor and test systems: Organizations must regularly monitor and test their systems to identify and address any security issues. This includes running regular scans and tests, and implementing corrective

measures to address any identified issues.

Explanation:

PCI DSS Requirement 8 is a crucial element of any Payment Card Industry Data Security Standard (PCI DSS) compliance program. It is designed to ensure that only authorized users have access to cardholder data, and that user access is monitored and managed appropriately. Requirement 8 states that organizations must identify and authenticate access to system components, and that access must be based on individual user's role. This means that access to cardholder data must be granted only to those users who have the necessary authority. Organizations must also ensure that appropriate access controls are in place to protect cardholder data from unauthorized access.

In order to meet Requirement 8, organizations must have a process in place to identify and authenticate access to system components. This can include using usernames and passwords, or using other methods of authentication such as biometrics or token-based authentication. Organizations must also ensure that users only have access to the data they need to do their job. Organizations must also ensure that user access is monitored and managed appropriately. This includes ensuring that users are only granted the least privilege necessary for their role, and that access is revoked promptly when no longer needed. Organizations must also ensure that user accounts are locked after a certain number of failed login attempts, and that users are required to change their passwords on a regular basis.

Finally, organizations must have a process in place to regularly review user access to system components. This includes reviewing user privileges and making sure they are appropriate for the user's role, and reviewing user accounts to ensure they are still in use. By complying with Requirement 8, organizations can ensure that access to cardholder data is secure and that only authorized users are able to access it. This helps to protect cardholder data from unauthorized access, and helps organizations to meet their PCI DSS compliance requirements.

CHAPTER 6

9. *Requirement 9 of the PCI DSS* is implement a process for identifying and managing security incidents: Organizations must have a process in place to identify and manage security incidents. This includes having an incident response plan and procedures in place to deal with incidents.

Explanation :

The Payment Card Industry Data Security Standard (PCI DSS) is a set of requirements designed to protect cardholder data and ensure the secure handling of payment card transactions. Requirement 9 of the PCI DSS focuses on the physical security of cardholder data. This requirement mandates that organizations take appropriate steps to protect cardholder data and to physically secure areas where cardholder data is stored, processed, or transmitted. This includes protecting all physical access to cardholder data and the devices used to process, store, or transmit it. The primary goal of Requirement 9 is to ensure that the environment in which data is stored and processed is secure. This involves the use of physical security measures such as locked doors, access control systems, video surveillance, and alarms.

Organizations must also designate and document physical access areas, as well as procedures for granting and revoking access. Access should also be limited to only those personnel who need it to perform their duties. Access control systems should be in place to monitor and document all access to data centers and other areas where cardholder data is stored or processed. Organizations must also use strong authentication methods, such as passwords, tokens, or biometrics, to control access to systems containing cardholder data. This includes systems used to store, process, or transmit cardholder data, as well as those used to manage the network and application infrastructure. Organizations must also perform regular tests of their physical security measures to ensure that they are effective. This includes testing the effectiveness of access control systems, video surveillance systems, and alarms. Organizations must also monitor logs and audit trails to detect and respond to any unauthorized access to cardholder data.

In addition, organizations must maintain an inventory of all physical devices, such as computers and servers, that are used to store, process, or transmit cardholder data. This inventory should include details such as the serial number, model number, and location of the device. Organizations must also ensure that media containing cardholder data is securely disposed of when it is no longer needed. This includes shredding, degaussing, or other methods of data destruction that render the data unrecoverable. By adhering to Requirement 9, organizations can ensure that their physical environment is secure and that cardholder data is adequately protected. This will help to minimize the risk of a data breach and help organizations comply with the PCI DSS.

10. *Requirement 10 of the PCI DSS* Ensure compliance with PCI DSS: Organizations must ensure that they are compliant with the PCI DSS. This includes regularly assessing the security of their systems and implementing corrective measures to address any non-compliant areas.

Explanation:

The Payment Card Industry Data Security Standard (PCI DSS) is a set of security standards developed by the major credit card companies to ensure the security of cardholder data. Requirement 10 of the PCI DSS is aimed at ensuring that cardholder data is adequately protected from malicious activity and unauthorized access. To comply with Requirement 10 of the PCI DSS, organizations must implement a comprehensive information security program that includes:

• *Restricting access to cardholder data*: Organizations must restrict access to cardholder data to only those individuals who need it to perform their job duties. Access to cardholder data must be based on an individual's role and must be granted on a need-to-know basis.

• *Establishing a secure network:* Organizations must establish and implement a secure data communications network that is protected from unauthorized access. This includes the use of firewalls, encryption, and other security measures to protect data in transit.

• *Maintaining a secure system*: Organizations must also maintain a secure system environment that is protected from malicious activity and unauthorized access. This includes the use of anti-virus software, spam filters, patch management systems, and intrusion detection systems.

• *Monitoring and testing*: Organizations must monitor and test their networks and systems on a regular basis to identify any potential security weaknesses. This includes periodic vulnerability scans and penetration tests.

• *Secure application development*: Organizations must ensure that any applications that are developed, purchased, or used within their environment are secure. This includes the use of secure coding standards and secure development processes.

• *Developing and implementing policy*: Organizations must develop and implement a written information security policy that outlines the organization's security requirements and procedures. This includes the use of acceptable use policies, access control policies, and incident response plans.

These requirements are essential to the security of cardholder data and must be met in order for organizations to comply with the PCI DSS. Failure to meet these requirements can result in fines, suspension of services, and other penalties from the credit card companies.

11.*Requirement 11 of the PCI DSS* Maintain an audit trail: Organizations must maintain an audit trail of all activities related to cardholder data. This includes logging access to cardholder data and regularly reviewing the logs.

Explanation:

The Payment Card Industry Data Security Standard (PCI DSS) is a set of security requirements designed to protect cardholders from the dangers of data breaches and identity theft. Requirement 11 of the PCI DSS is focused on testing and monitoring the security of the cardholder data environment (CDE). This requirement is designed to ensure that the CDE is constantly monitored so that any changes or threats can be identified and addressed in a timely manner. Requirement 11 consists of four distinct sub-requirements. First, organizations must perform periodic internal and external vulnerability scans on the CDE. This process involves scanning the system to identify any potential threats and vulnerabilities. Organizations must also ensure that any identified vulnerabilities are addressed promptly. Second, organizations must perform periodic penetration testing of the CDE. Penetration testing is a process in which a third-party security expert attempts to gain unauthorized access to the system. The results of these tests must be reported to the organization and any identified vulnerabilities must be addressed. Third, organizations must monitor and analyze all access to the CDE. This includes tracking all user access, system changes, and any other activities that could potentially compromise the security of the system. Organizations must also ensure that any access attempts that could potentially lead to unauthorized access are blocked immediately. Finally, organizations must maintain an audit log of all activities related to the CDE. This includes user access, system changes, and any other activities that could potentially compromise the security of the system. Organizations must also ensure that the audit log is reviewed regularly and any suspicious activities are investigated promptly.

Overall, Requirement 11 of the PCI DSS is designed to ensure that organizations are constantly testing and monitoring the security of the CDE. Organizations must conduct regular vulnerability scans, penetration tests, monitor user access, and maintain an audit log of all activities related to the CDE. By adhering to these requirements, organizations can reduce their risk of suffering a data breach or identity theft.

CHAPTER 7

12. *Requirement 12 of the PCI DSS* Maintain a program to manage service providers: Organizations must have a program in place to manage service providers who have access to cardholder data. This includes regularly assessing the security of service providers and implementing corrective measures to address any identified issues.

Explanation:

The Payment Card Industry Data Security Standard (PCI DSS) is a set of security requirements designed to ensure the secure handling of payment card information. Requirement 12 is focused on ensuring the secure management of authentication credentials. Authentication Credentials are the methods used to prove a user's identity when accessing systems, networks, or applications. Authentication credentials are typically used to gain access to sensitive systems, networks, or applications and can include usernames, passwords, biometric scans, or security tokens. Requirement 12 of the PCI DSS requires organizations to implement controls to protect authentication credentials and limit access to sensitive systems, networks, and applications. Organizations must develop and implement secure procedures to manage authentication credentials, including procedures for creating, changing, and protecting credentials, and for assigning and managing roles and privileges. Organizations must also restrict access to authentication credentials to only those individuals who have a legitimate business need to access the system, network, or application. They must also implement controls to ensure that authentication credentials are not shared or reused. Organizations must also implement procedures to detect and respond to any unauthorized use of authentication credentials. This includes monitoring for any attempts to use default or weak credentials, monitoring for any attempts to use authentication credentials from terminated employees, and responding to any attempts to use authentication credentials from unauthorized users. Finally, organizations must document all authentication credentials and associated privileges, and must review and update these credentials and privileges on a regular basis.

In summary, Requirement 12 of the PCI DSS is focused on ensuring secure management of authentication credentials. Organizations must develop and implement secure procedures to manage and protect authentication credentials, must limit access to these credentials to only those individuals who have a legitimate business need to access the system, network, or application, and must document and review authentication credentials on a regular basis.

CHAPTER 8

3. Creating a Data Security Policy

What is a data security policy?

A data security policy is a set of guidelines and practices implemented by organizations to protect their data from unauthorized access. It specifies the type of data that can and cannot be accessed, how it should be used and stored, and who is responsible for ensuring the security of the data. It applies to the entire organization, including employees, vendors, and customers. Data security policies are essential for ensuring the proper handling of sensitive information, such as customer data, financial information, and other confidential data. They can help to protect against data breaches, privacy violations, and other security threats. The most important element of a data security policy is the clear definition of who can access the data and under what circumstances. Access to sensitive data should be restricted to only those that have a legitimate need for it, such as employees with specific roles or those with access granted by the organization. Policies should also specify how data should be stored and secured, such as using encryption and authentication methods to protect data. Organizations should also ensure that there is a process for monitoring and responding to data security incidents, such as unauthorized access or attempts to breach the system. It should include a detailed response plan and steps to investigate and remediate the issue.

A data security policy should also include guidelines for employees on how to handle data securely. This includes proper handling of passwords and other sensitive information, as well as how to securely store and share data. Organizations should also provide training to employees on the importance of data security and how to protect it. Data security policies are essential for protecting an organization's data and ensuring that it is handled securely. They apply to everyone in the organization, from employees to vendors and customers, and should be regularly reviewed and updated to ensure they are up to date and still meet the organization's needs. Data security policies are an important aspect of any organization's security infrastructure. They provide a clear framework for protecting your sensitive data, ensuring that it is used responsibly and in accordance with your company's security standards. Establishing a data security policy is critical for any organization, regardless of size.

When creating a data security policy, it is important to consider the needs of your organization and the data that needs to be protected. First, determine the types of data that your organization handles and the potential risks associated with that data. This includes identifying any sensitive data, such as financial or personal information, and any regulatory requirements that may apply. Once you have identified the types of data that need to be protected, it is important to establish clear guidelines for how this data should be handled. This includes protocols for access control, authentication, encryption, and logging. These protocols should be detailed in your policy and should be regularly reviewed and updated to ensure that they remain current with changing technologies and threats. In addition to access control protocols, you should also define guidelines for how your data should be stored. This includes specifying the locations where data should be stored, the type of storage media that should be used, and any specific policies for data backup and recovery. It is also important to define the roles and responsibilities of each team member regarding data security.

This includes outlining the specific roles and duties of each team member, as well as who is responsible for monitoring and enforcing the data security policy.

Finally, it is important to establish a process for responding to data security incidents. This includes specifying the procedures for reporting a security incident, determining the severity of the incident, and taking the appropriate action to mitigate the risk. Creating a comprehensive data security policy helps ensure that your data is secure and that your team members are aware of their responsibility for protecting it. By following the steps outlined above, you can create a robust policy that will keep your data safe and secure.How to create a data security policy? Data security is a hot topic in the world today. With the prevalence of cybercrime, organizations must take steps to ensure their data is secure. One way to do this is to create a data security policy. This policy will outline the steps that a company must take to protect its data from unauthorized access, destruction and manipulation.

The first step in creating a data security policy is to identify the types of data that need to be secured. This includes not only customer or employee information, but also any sensitive financial or proprietary information. Once the data types have been identified, the organization must determine who needs access to this data, and the level of access they need. This step is important for ensuring that only those with a legitimate need have access to the data. The next step is to develop the policy itself. The policy should clearly state who has access to the data, and what level of access they have. It should also outline the procedures for securely storing and transferring data, as well as the steps that should be taken if a breach occurs. A policy should also include a section on user training, to ensure that all users are aware of the organization's data security procedures. Once the policy has been created, it should be regularly reviewed and updated as needed. New technologies, such as cloud storage, can create new vulnerabilities, and the policy should be updated to ensure that the organization is keeping up with the latest security trends.

Creating a data security policy is an important step in keeping an organization's data safe from unauthorized access. By taking the time to identify the types of data that need to be secured, and then outlining the procedures for keeping it secure, organizations can protect their data and ensure that it remains safe.

CHAPTER 9

4. *Exploring Common Security Threats*

Security threats are a major concern for businesses in the modern world. With the ever-evolving nature of technology, it is becoming increasingly difficult to keep up with the latest threats and protect against them. In this article, we will discuss some of the most common security threats in today's digital landscape.

Malware:

Malware is a term for malicious software, which is used to damage or gain unauthorized access to a computer system. Malware can be used for a variety of malicious activities, including stealing information, taking control of a system, and disrupting services. Malware is often spread through email, social media links, and malicious websites. Malware comes in many forms, including viruses, worms, trojan horses, ransomware, and spyware. Viruses are malicious programs that can infect your computer and spread to other computers. Worms are similar to viruses, but they spread without any user intervention. Trojan horses are malicious programs that masquerade as legitimate applications, but are actually malicious programs that can cause damage or steal information. Ransomware is malicious software that takes control of a computer and demands payment in order to release the computer. Spyware is software that is installed without the user's knowledge and is used to track the user's activity and steal information.

The best way to protect yourself from malware is to use a reputable antivirus program and keep it up to date. You should also keep your operating system and other software up to date with the latest security patches. Additionally, you should be cautious when downloading software from the internet, especially from untrusted sources. Finally, you should back up your data regularly to protect against data loss due to malware. There are many ways that malware can be used to damage or gain unauthorized access to a computer system. It is important to be aware of the different types of malware and take steps to protect your computer from malicious software. By taking the necessary precautions, you can help protect yourself and your data from malicious software.

Malware is one of the most common security threats. Malware is malicious software that can be used to gain access to a system without the user's knowledge. It can be used to steal data, install ransomware, or even take control of the system. Malware can be spread through email attachments, downloads, and even through malicious websites.

Phishing:

Phishing is a type of cyber attack that uses social engineering techniques to steal personal information and data from unsuspecting victims. It typically involves an attacker sending a malicious email, text message, or social media message that appears to be from a legitimate source, such as a bank or other financial institution. The message will typically contain a link that leads to a spoofed website designed to look like the legitimate site, where the victim is asked to enter personal information such as account numbers, passwords, or credit card numbers. Phishing attacks have become increasingly sophisticated, often using techniques such as spoofed email addresses, malicious attachments, and malicious URLs. Attackers often use social engineering techniques to craft messages that appear to be from legitimate organizations or individuals, making them difficult to detect. To protect against phishing attacks, it is important to be aware of the signs of a potential phishing attack. Any email or message that requests personal information should be treated with suspicion. It is also important to be aware of the content of the message, as attackers may use scare tactics or false promises to lure victims into providing their information. Additionally, links should be examined before clicking, as malicious links can be used to take victims to spoofed sites.

Finally, it is important to use a secure web browser and anti-phishing software, as this can help detect and block malicious messages. Additionally, it is important to use strong passwords, as weak passwords can be easily guessed by attackers and used to gain access to accounts. By following these steps, individuals can reduce the risk of becoming a victim of a phishing attack. Phishing is another common security threat. Phishing is a type of social engineering attack where attackers use deceptive emails, fake websites, and other methods to try to get users to give up their login credentials or other sensitive information. The aim is to steal money or data, or to gain access to the user's system.

Ransomware:

Another security threat is ransomware. Ransomware is a type of malicious software (malware) designed to block access to a computer system or its data until a ransom is paid. It is typically spread through phishing emails or by unknowingly visiting an infected website. Once the ransomware is downloaded, it will encrypt the files on the system and demand payment in exchange for the decryption key that will allow access to the data. Ransomware is a growing threat that can have devastating consequences for individuals and businesses. It is estimated that ransomware attacks cost organizations an average of $133,000 per incident. Additionally, data encrypted by ransomware can be permanently lost if the attacker does not provide the decryption key.

There are several types of ransomware, including lockers, which lock users out of their systems, and crypto-ransomware, which encrypts files and requires payment for the decryption key. Other types of ransomware include wiper, which deletes files, and screen lockers, which display a message on the infected computer's screen. It is important to take steps to protect against ransomware attacks. This includes keeping all software and operating systems up to date, using strong passwords, and avoiding suspicious emails and websites. Additionally, having a backup of all important data in a secure location can help minimize the impact of a ransomware attack. It is also important to be aware of the warning signs of a ransomware attack. These include sudden changes to system settings, suspicious emails or websites, and strange messages that appear on the screen. It is also important to remember that paying the ransom does not guarantee that the attacker will provide the decryption key.

By taking the necessary precautions, individuals and businesses can protect themselves against ransomware attacks and minimize the potential damage they can cause. Ransomware is a type of malicious software designed to lock down a computer or network and hold it hostage until the user pays a ransom. It can be spread through email attachments, downloads, and even through malicious websites.

DDoS:

Finally, Distributed Denial of Service (DDoS) attacks are becoming increasingly common. DDoS attacks are designed to overwhelm a system with traffic, making it difficult or impossible for the system to respond. DDoS attacks can be used to take down websites, disrupt services, or even steal data. A Distributed Denial of Service (DDoS) attack is a malicious cyber attack used to bring down a network or website by overwhelming it with traffic from multiple sources. It is one of the most common cyber attacks used today and can have devastating effects on a business or organization. DDoS attacks are typically launched by a group of malicious actors, referred to as "botmasters" or "hackers." These botmasters typically gain control of a network of computers, known as a botnet, and use them to launch an attack. The idea is to send so much traffic to the target server or website that it becomes overwhelmed and unable to respond. This can cause websites to crash, networks to become unreachable, and can even take down entire networks. DDoS attacks can be targeted at a variety of different resources, such as web servers, application servers, and databases. The attacks can also vary in complexity, from a single attack aimed at a single server, to a larger attack aimed at multiple targets across the internet.

In addition to the technical complexity of the attack, DDoS attacks can also vary in the amount of disruption they cause. The most disruptive attacks are those that take down entire networks, while smaller attacks may only cause limited disruption. Fortunately, there are steps businesses and organizations can take to protect themselves from DDoS attacks. These include implementing firewalls, utilizing DDoS mitigation systems, and ensuring that networks are up-to-date with the latest security patches. Additionally, businesses and organizations should regularly monitor their networks for any suspicious activity that may indicate a DDoS attack is in progress.

Overall, DDoS attacks are a serious threat to businesses and organizations. While there is no single solution to protect against these attacks, there are steps that can be taken to minimize their impact and ensure that networks stay secure. These are just a few of the most common security threats businesses must be aware of. It is important to stay up to date on the latest threats and to take steps to protect your business. This includes implementing strong security measures, monitoring for suspicious activity, and training employees on how to recognize and respond to potential threats.

CHAPTER 10

Implementing Encryption Technologies

What is encryption technology?

Encryption technology is one of the most effective and efficient ways to protect data from malicious attacks and unauthorized access. It is used in a variety of applications, from securing financial transactions to protecting confidential medical and business records. It is important to understand the fundamentals of encryption technology in order to be able to make informed decisions about security and privacy. Encryption technology works by transforming data into a form that is unreadable to anyone without the correct key. This transformation is typically accomplished with an algorithm, which is a mathematical formula that is used to scramble the data. A specific key is then used to unscramble the data, allowing only those with the key to access the data. Two main types of encryption technology exist. The first is symmetric encryption, which requires the same key to encrypt and decrypt data. This type of encryption is commonly used for web transactions, as it is relatively secure. The second type of encryption is asymmetric encryption, which uses two separate keys to encrypt and decrypt data. This type of encryption is more secure and is typically used for highly sensitive data, such as banking details.

Encryption technology also comes in different levels of complexity. For example, some encryption algorithms are more secure than others, meaning that it is more difficult to decrypt data that is encrypted with a more complex algorithm.

Additionally, different types of encryption require different levels of computing power in order to decrypt the data. In addition to protecting data from malicious attacks and unauthorized access, encryption technology can also be used to validate data integrity. This means that it is possible to verify that the data has not been tampered with or otherwise altered before it is sent or received. In short, encryption technology is an essential tool for protecting data from malicious attacks and unauthorized access. It is important to understand the fundamentals of encryption technology in order to make informed decisions about security and privacy. Additionally, it is important to select a secure encryption algorithm and to ensure that the appropriate computing power is available to decrypt the data.

Encryption technology is one of the most effective methods of protecting data. It is a process which encodes data so that it cannot be accessed without a key. In today's digital world, encryption technology is becoming increasingly important for businesses and individuals to protect their data and secure their communications. In this article, we will discuss how to implement encryption technology.

1. *Choose an encryption algorithm*: The first step in implementing encryption technology is to choose an appropriate encryption algorithm. There are various types of encryption algorithms, each with their own strengths and weaknesses. For example, symmetric encryption algorithms are faster and simpler to implement, while asymmetric algorithms are more secure but more complex to set up. It is important to carefully evaluate the encryption algorithm that best meets your needs.

2. *Generate a key*: Once you have chosen an encryption algorithm, the next step is to generate a strong encryption key. A strong key is essential for protecting against brute-force attacks, which are attempts to guess your key by trying all possible combinations. To generate a strong key, use a key generation tool which combines random characters, numbers, and symbols.

3. *Implement the encryption*: Once you have chosen your encryption algorithm and generated a strong key, you can begin to implement the encryption technology. This involves writing code which uses the encryption algorithm and key to encrypt and decrypt data. If you are not experienced in coding, you may need to hire a programmer to help you with this step.

4. *Test the encryption*: After you have implemented the encryption technology, it is important to test it to make sure it is working correctly. You can do this by using a test suite to encrypt and decrypt data and verifying that the results are correct.

5. *Monitor the encryption*: Finally, it is important to regularly monitor your encryption technology to ensure it is still working correctly and not vulnerable to attack. You should also keep an eye out for any new developments or vulnerabilities in encryption algorithms and update your system accordingly.

By following these steps, you should be able to implement encryption technology effectively and securely. Encryption technology is an essential tool for protecting data and communications in the digital age, and is well worth the effort to set up and maintain.

Conducting Security Audits and Vulnerability Scans

Security audits and vulnerability scans are two of the most important elements of any organization's cyber security strategy. They help organizations identify and mitigate security risks, protect their network and data, and ensure that their systems meet compliance requirements. Security audits are comprehensive assessments of an organization's overall security posture. Auditors will analyze an organization's systems, policies, procedures, and security controls to identify potential vulnerabilities and areas of improvement. This process typically includes a detailed review of an organization's security policies and procedures, as well as its compliance with laws and regulations. The goal of a security audit is to help organizations identify weaknesses and potential risks, and to help them develop an effective security strategy to reduce those risks.

Vulnerability scans are an important part of any security audit. These scans are designed to detect weaknesses in an organization's network, systems, and applications that could be exploited by malicious actors. Vulnerability scans typically involve the use of automated tools to identify potential weaknesses in an organization's security posture. These scans help organizations identify and prioritize areas of risk, and can be used to develop effective security measures to address those risks.

CHAPTER 11

What is are vulnerabilities?

A vulnerability scan is an automated process that checks a computer system for known security weaknesses. It is a form of security assessment used to identify, analyze, and report any potential security risks or vulnerabilities that exist in a computer system or network. Vulnerability scans are typically performed by a security professional or an automated program. Vulnerability scans can help organizations identify security risks and take preemptive steps to prevent potential attacks. By scanning a computer system or network, an organization can identify security holes before malicious actors exploit them. A vulnerability scan looks for known security vulnerabilities, such as weak passwords, unpatched software, misconfigured systems, and other potential security issues. Vulnerability scans are typically performed using a variety of tools and techniques, such as port scanning, vulnerability scanning, and web application scanning. Port scanning involves scanning a system's open ports, which are points of access for data or commands. Vulnerability scanning looks for known weaknesses in the system, such as outdated software or weak authentication protocols. Web application scanning looks for security flaws in web applications, such as SQL injection flaws or Cross-Site Scripting (XSS) vulnerabilities.

Vulnerability scans are a critical component of any security program and can help organizations identify and address potential security risks before they become a problem. By regularly performing vulnerability scans, organizations can ensure that their systems are secure and compliant with industry standards. Both security audits and vulnerability scans are essential elements of any organization's cyber security strategy. They can help organizations identify and mitigate security risks, protect their networks and data, and ensure that their systems meet compliance requirements. By conducting regular security audits and vulnerability scans, organizations can ensure that their cyber security posture is up-to-date and in line with industry standards.

How to conduct security audits?

PCI Security Auditing is a process of assessing the compliance of a company's information security systems with the Payment Card Industry (PCI) Data Security Standard (DSS). The PCI DSS is a set of security guidelines created by the Payment Card Industry Security Council (PCI Council) to protect cardholder data on the payment networks. As such, all organizations that store, process, or transmit payment card data are required to adhere to the PCI DSS.

A PCI security audit is a comprehensive process that evaluates an organization's compliance with the PCI DSS. The audit includes an assessment of the organization's security policies, procedures, and practices, as well as the technical aspects of the system. The following are the steps to conducting a PCI security audit:

1. Determine the Scope of the Audit: The first step in conducting a PCI security audit is to determine the scope of the audit. This includes identifying which systems, procedures, and practices need to be evaluated. It is important to note that the scope of the audit must include all systems and processes that handle cardholder data.

2. Assess the Organization's Security Policies and Practices: The second step in a PCI security audit is to assess the organization's security policies and practices. This includes evaluating the security measures that the organization has implemented to protect cardholder data, such as encryption and access control measures. It is also important to assess the organization's process for responding to security incidents.

3. Evaluate the Technical Aspects of the System: The third step in a PCI security audit is to evaluate the technical aspects of the system. This includes assessing the system's security architecture, network configuration, and software security. It is also important to evaluate the system's patch management and log management processes.

4. Document the Audit Process: The fourth step in a PCI security audit is to document the audit process. This includes documenting the scope of the audit, the assessment of the organization's security policies and practices, and the evaluation of the technical aspects of the system. It is also important to document any non-compliant areas that were identified during the audit.

5. Report the Results: The fifth step in a PCI security audit is to report the results of the audit. This includes providing the organization with a report that outlines the findings of the audit, as well as any recommendations for improving the system's security.

PCI security auditing is an important process that all organizations that store, process, or transmit payment card data must adhere to. By following the steps outlined above, organizations can ensure that their systems are compliant with the PCI DSS and that cardholder data is secure.

CHAPTER 12

How to perform a vulnerability?

A vulnerability scan is an important part of keeping your network secure. It is a process of scanning a system or network for potential weaknesses that could be exploited by malicious actors. Vulnerability scans can identify and help patch security flaws before a breach occurs.The first step in performing a vulnerability scan is to identify the assets to be scanned. This involves gathering information about the network infrastructure and assets such as computers, servers, and other connected devices. It is important to determine which assets are critical and should be scanned more frequently. Next, you will need to select a scanning tool. There are many different types of vulnerability scanners available including open source and commercial solutions. Open source tools are free to download and use, but may require more configuration and expertise to use effectively. Commercial tools are often easier to configure and use, but can be expensive.

Once the scanning tool is selected, you will need to configure it to scan the network. This involves setting the scan parameters and configuring the type of scan to be performed. Different scanners offer different types of scans, such as port scans and application scans. An experienced network administrator should be able to configure the scanner to scan for the most common types of vulnerabilities. Once the scan is configured, it can be run. Depending on the size of the network and the type of scan being performed, this process may take some time. It is important to ensure that the scanning process does not interfere with normal network operations. Once the scan is complete, the results will be displayed. This will show any potential vulnerabilities that were detected. It is important to review the results carefully and take action to remediate any vulnerabilities that were detected.

In summary, performing a vulnerability scan is an important part of maintaining a secure network. It involves identifying the assets to be scanned, selecting a scanning tool, configuring the scan parameters, running the scan, and reviewing the results. Taking the time to properly perform vulnerability scans can help to ensure that any security flaws are identified and patched before they can be exploited.

7. Understanding the Reporting Requirements

Explanation:

The Payment Card Industry Data Security Standard (PCI DSS) was created to provide a secure environment for businesses to process and store cardholder data. As part of this security standard, businesses must adhere to a set of reporting requirements that ensure they are protecting their customers' data and complying with the PCI DSS. The first reporting requirement is that businesses must submit a Self-Assessment Questionnaire (SAQ) to their acquirer or payment brand annually. This questionnaire is used to assess the business's compliance with the PCI DSS. It includes questions about the business's security policies and procedures, as well as its cardholder data environment. The second reporting requirement is that businesses must submit an Attestation of Compliance (AOC) to their acquirer or payment brand annually. This document is used to certify that the business has met the PCI DSS requirements and is compliant. It must be signed by an authorized representative of the business and submitted to the acquirer or payment brand.

The third reporting requirement is that businesses must submit a Report on Compliance (ROC) to their acquirer or payment brand annually. The ROC is used to provide an independent assessment of the business's compliance with the PCI DSS. It must be completed by an independent qualified security assessor (QSA) who is approved by the payment brand. The fourth reporting requirement is that businesses must submit any required evidence of compliance to their acquirer or payment brand annually. This evidence may include test results, policies, procedures, or other documentation that demonstrate the business is compliant with the PCI DSS.

How to perform reporting requirements.

PCI DSS (Payment Card Industry Data Security Standard) is a set of security standards intended to protect the security of payment card data. It is a set of requirements that all merchants and service providers who process, store, or transmit cardholder data must adhere to. The Payment Card Industry Security Standards Council (PCI SSC) is responsible for developing and maintaining these standards. In order to comply with PCI DSS, organizations must meet certain reporting requirements. These requirements include submitting periodic reports to demonstrate that they are adhering to the standards and that their systems remain secure. This article will provide an overview of the PCI DSS reporting requirements and how organizations can comply with them.

The first step in meeting the PCI DSS reporting requirements is to create a Self-Assessment Questionnaire (SAQ). This questionnaire is designed to assess an organization's security posture. It consists of various questions related to the organization's systems and processes, and the answers to these questions are used to determine how well the organization is complying with the PCI DSS standards. Organizations should complete the SAQ at least annually in order to ensure that their security posture is up to date and that their systems remain secure. The second step is to submit a Report on Compliance (ROC). This report must be submitted to the PCI SSC on an annual basis. The ROC must include the results of the organization's SAQ as well as any other relevant information such as system changes or security incidents. The ROC is used by the PCI SSC to assess an organization's compliance with the PCI DSS standards and to determine if any corrective action needs to be taken. The third step is to submit an Attestation of Compliance (AoC). This document is an additional report that must be submitted to the PCI SSC every 12 months. The AoC must include the results of the organization's SAQ as well as any other relevant information such as system changes or security incidents. The AoC is used by the PCI SSC to assess an organization's compliance with the PCI DSS standards and to determine if any corrective action needs to be taken.

These three steps are essential for any organization that is required to comply with the PCI DSS standards. By following these steps, organizations can ensure that their systems remain secure and that they are meeting the reporting requirements of the PCI DSS. By adhering to these reporting requirements, businesses can ensure they are meeting the PCI DSS requirements and protecting their customers' data. Failing to comply with these requirements can result in non-compliance penalties and fines, so it is important that businesses understand and adhere to them.

CHAPTER 13

Penalties for Non-Compliance

The Payment Card Industry Data Security Standard (PCI DSS) is a set of security standards designed to protect cardholder data when processing, storing, and transmitting credit card information. Non-compliance with the PCI DSS is a serious offense and can result in hefty fines, as well as other serious repercussions.

Fines

The PCI Security Standards Council (PCI SSC) is responsible for setting the standards for PCI DSS compliance. The PCI SSC is also responsible for enforcing the standards, and merchants who are found to be non-compliant can face a variety of penalties.The most common penalty for non-compliance is a fine from the credit card companies. The exact amount of the fine depends on the severity of the violation, as well as the size of the merchant. Generally, the fines range from $5,000 to $100,000 per month for non-compliance.

Loss of Credit Card Privileges

In addition to fines, non-compliant merchants may also have their credit card processing privileges revoked. This means that the merchant will no longer be able to accept credit cards from customers, which can have a serious impact on their business.

Regulatory Enforcement

The PCI SSC is also able to take action against non-compliant merchants by referring the matter to regulatory authorities. Depending on the severity of the violation, the merchant may face criminal charges or be subject to a civil lawsuit.

Reputational Damage

Non-compliance with the PCI DSS can also have a negative impact on the merchant's reputation. Customers may be unwilling to do business with the merchant if they know that their credit card data is not being properly safeguarded.

The Payment Card Industry Data Security Standard (PCI DSS) is an information security standard issued by the PCI Security Standards Council to protect organizations and their customers from data breaches involving credit and debit card information. It is a set of security requirements that all organizations that process, store or transmit cardholder data must adhere to. Unfortunately, many organizations do not comply with these requirements, resulting in hefty penalties from the PCI Security Standards Council.

Companies that have been penalized for non compliant?

One example of a company that was penalized for non-compliance with PCI DSS is Target. In 2013, Target was the victim of a massive data breach that affected more than 40 million customers. As part of the investigation, the PCI Security Standards Council found that Target had failed to comply with PCI DSS. As a result, the company was fined $18.5 million by the Payment Card Industry Security Standards Council.

Another example of a company penalized for not complying with PCI DSS is Home Depot. In 2014, Home Depot announced that its payment systems had been breached, resulting in the theft of credit and debit card information from millions of customers. The PCI Security Standards Council found Home Depot guilty of not complying with PCI DSS requirements, and the company was fined $19.5 million. In addition to Target and Home Depot, several other companies have been penalized for not complying with PCI DSS. These include Neiman Marcus, Michaels Stores, TJX Companies, and Heartland Payment Systems. Each of these companies was fined millions of dollars for failing to adhere to the PCI DSS requirements. It is important for companies to take the PCI DSS requirements seriously and ensure that they are adhered to. Failing to do so can result in hefty fines and reputational damage. Companies should make sure they are compliant with PCI DSS and have the necessary security measures in place to protect customer data.

In conclusion, non-compliance with the PCI DSS can have serious consequences. Merchants should take steps to ensure they are in compliance with the standards, or risk facing fines, the loss of credit card privileges, regulatory enforcement, and reputational damage.

CONCLUSION

Conclusion

The Payment Card Industry Data Security Standard (PCI DSS) has become a widely accepted standard for ensuring the security of payment card information and is used by millions of companies worldwide. As the e-commerce industry continues to grow and evolve, so too does the need to protect customer data and ensure the security of online payments. As such, the future of PCI DSS is one of continued importance and growth. As technology advances, so too do the threats to payment card data. Cyber criminals are becoming more sophisticated in their attacks, and the need for more secure payment systems is becoming increasingly important. PCI DSS is continuously being updated to address evolving threats and provide the highest level of security for companies that accept payment cards. In addition to providing a secure payment system, PCI DSS is also becoming increasingly important for companies to comply with various government regulations. Many governments have implemented laws and regulations requiring companies to adhere to data security standards, and PCI DSS is often used as the basis for these regulations. As such, companies that accept payment cards must adhere to PCI DSS in order to remain compliant with government regulations.

The future of PCI DSS also includes the development of new technologies and tools to help companies better protect their customer data. For example, tokenization and point-to-point encryption (P2PE) are two technologies that are becoming increasingly popular for protecting customer data. Tokenization replaces payment card information with a unique token, while

P2PE encrypts payment card data as it is being sent from a customer to a merchant. These technologies can help reduce the risk of data breaches and ensure that customers' payment card information remains safe.

nvvj   In short, the future of PCI DSS is one of continued importance and growth. As technology advances, so too does the need for secure payment systems, and PCI DSS provides a framework for doing just that. New technologies and tools are also being developed to help companies better protect their customer data, and governments are continuing to require companies to adhere to data security standards. As such, companies that accept payment cards must ensure they are in compliance with PCI DSS to remain compliant with government regulations and protect their customers' payment card data.

ABOUT THE AUTHOR

About the Author:

Ethan Damitier, the author of "Secure Transactions: The Fundamentals of PCI DSS," is a recognized expert in the field of cybersecurity and payment card security. With a passion for helping organizations navigate the complex landscape of data protection and compliance, [Your Name] has dedicated their career to promoting secure practices in the digital realm.

Drawing upon Ethan's extensive experience in the industry, which spans over many years, he has developed a deep understanding of the challenges businesses face when it comes to safeguarding sensitive cardholder data and meeting regulatory requirements. His expertise extends beyond theoretical knowledge, as he has worked closely with organizations from various sectors, assisting them in achieving and maintaining PCI DSS compliance.

Ethan's professional journey started with a solid educational foundation in cybersecurity and information technology. He holds advanced degrees in the field and have continually pursued professional development to stay at the forefront of emerging trends and evolving security practices. His deep technical knowledge is complemented by a strong business acumen, allowing them to bridge the gap between technology and organizational objectives.

Throughout his career, Ethan Damitier has worked with both small businesses and large enterprises, offering consulting services, conducting security assessments, and developing robust security strategies. His commitment to helping organizations navigate the intricacies of PCI DSS compliance and establish a culture of security has earned them a reputation as a trusted advisor and thought leader in the industry.

As an author, Ethan Damitier is dedicated to sharing his knowledge and expertise with a wider audience. He understand the importance of accessible and practical resources in helping organizations effectively implement security measures. Through his writing, he aims to demystify complex concepts, break down regulatory requirements, and empower readers with the tools and insights necessary to protect their customers' data and build a secure transaction environment. In addition to his professional pursuits, Ethan Damitier actively contributes to industry associations, participates in security conferences, and engages in knowledge-sharing initiatives. He firmly believe in the power of collaboration and the continuous exchange of ideas to drive advancements in the field of cybersecurity.

"Secure Transactions: The Fundamentals of PCI DSS" is a culmination of Ethan Damitier's expertise, passion, and dedication to helping organizations navigate the world of payment card security. It reflects their commitment to empowering businesses, professionals, and security enthusiasts with the knowledge and best practices needed to ensure the integrity of payment transactions and protect sensitive cardholder data.

Through this book, Ethan invites you to join him on a journey towards a more secure future, where organizations can confidently navigate the complexities of PCI DSS compliance and build trust with their customers.